A jug decorated with scenes of 'The Sailor's Return' and 'The Sailor's Farewell'. The glaze is heavily tinted with cobalt. Impressed PRATT on the base. Made by William Pratt at Lane Delph; c.1790. Height 155 mm.

PRATT WARE
An introduction

John and Griselda Lewis

Shire Publications Ltd

CONTENTS

Printed in Great Britain by CIT Printing Services, Press Buildings, Merlins Bridge, Haverfordwest, Dyfed SA61 1XF.

British Library Cataloguing in Publication Data: Lewis, John. Pratt Ware: An Introduction - (Shire Albums; No. 296). I. Title II. Lewis, Griselda III. Series 738.3. ISBN 0-7478-0220-3.

Cover: An octagonal jug with scenes in relief with underglaze colours of 'The Sailor's Return' and 'The Sailor's Farewell' on either side; c.1790. Height 180 mm.

ACKNOWLEDGEMENTS
Photographs are from private collections, except those on pages 12 (top right) and 19 (bottom), which are reproduced by courtesy of Elias Clark, and page 24 (bottom), by courtesy of Sotheby's.

The PRATT mark, impressed on the base of 'The Sailor's Return' jug. The lemon-shaped footrim is a noticeable feature of jugs made by the Pratts.

Left: *The commonest of the commemorative underglaze-coloured relief-decorated jugs with portraits of Admiral Nelson on one side and Captain Berry on the other, their names moulded in relief. Probably made at the Leeds Pottery after the battle of the Nile; c.1797. Height 191 mm.*

Right: *A jug with 'The Sailor's Return' on one side and 'Britannia' on the other. This example is unmarked, but there is an identical version of this jug with the PRATT mark on it; c.1790. Height 140 mm.*

INTRODUCTION

Pratt ware (a term coined by the potter G. Woolliscroft Rhead in 1909) is the name given to relief-decorated underglaze-coloured earthenware made from about 1780 to 1840 in England and Scotland. It is a misnomer, for contemporary potters referred to underglazed ware of this kind as 'painted ware'. Wares coloured over the glaze were called 'enamelled ware'. In the mid eighteenth century much pottery was decorated with coloured glazes. The use of underglaze colouring came in only towards the end of the era and before the more expensive enamel colouring became popular.

The last two decades of the eighteenth century and the first of the nineteenth were troubled times. The threat of war with France encouraged patriotic fervour. The makers of relief-decorated underglaze-coloured earthenware were not slow to take advantage of this, for they made many commemorative pieces showing portraits of royalty and popular heroes of the time.

Much of the charm of underglaze-coloured ware lies in the restricted palette, which was limited to oxide colours: lead, tin and antimony for yellow, with the addition of iron oxide for deeper yellow and orange; cobalt for blue; lead and copper for greens; iron oxide with the addition of manganese for browns. Manganese oxide by itself made a purplish brown. Black was made by mixing iron oxide and cobalt. The rich mulberry colour or puce on some pieces was made by using chloride of manganese with oxides of iron and manganese.

These oxides were painted on to the biscuit body, which was then lead-glazed and fired to between 1000°C and 1100°C. These colours were able to withstand the heat necessary for fusing the glaze. Because only one additional firing was needed after the biscuit firing, the ware was relatively cheap to produce, unlike the later and more highly coloured enamelled ware, which needed several firings.

3

Many of the enamel colours had to be fired separately in a low-temperature muffle kiln.

The ware itself is easily recognisable and is unlike anything else. The actual body of the pieces varies. Much of it is extremely good-quality creamware, often with a slightly blue-tinted glaze, achieved by the addition of small quantities of cobalt. This gave the ware a whiteness not obtainable with a lead glaze, which has a faint yellow tinge. Some of the ware is made from a drab, putty-coloured body and this is less attractive.

The jugs, mugs, teapots and so on were all press-moulded, as slip casting, except for stoneware, was not possible at that time. The quality of the raised decoration can vary from beautifully crisp pieces pressed from new moulds to less well-defined designs pressed from worn moulds. The quality of the painting also varies, from carefully decorated examples to smeary slapdash painting that was probably done by child labour.

The ware was made for a relatively unsophisticated market. Apart from the commemorative pieces, much of the ware is decorated with rural scenes, birds and animals and all kinds of country sports including hunting, shooting, archery, racing and coursing. Drinking was also a very popular subject. Classical designs were used on the more sophisticated pieces such as teapots.

The subjects used for decoration were copied either from contemporary prints in the popular journals of the day, or from Wedgwood's jasper-ware sprigged designs, or from the glass portraits by James and William Tassie. James Tassie, after studying drawing and modelling at the Foulis Academy in Glasgow, went over to Dublin and there learnt to make casts in a white glass paste. He was joined by his nephew William, who made a glass-paste portrait of Admiral Duncan which was copied on to various Pratt jugs and flasks.

Some of the rural scenes, and especially those featuring children, were adapted from drawings by Lady Templetown and Lady Diana Beauclerk, who both produced designs for the Wedgwood factory at Etruria.

Jugs are the commonest pieces to be found. Some of the designs were made in sets of three or five sizes, or even more. Mugs are more difficult to find. They would have been in constant use and therefore many more would have been broken. There are a great many Toby jugs decorated with underglaze colours. Teapots are not common and are often of a very good quality. Plaques must have been popular, for there are many of them still surviving.

Figures and busts were produced in some quantity. The small early press-moulded 'toys' were often made by children who worked long hours for pathetically small wages. These little figures were decorated with haphazard spots and blobs of colour, nearly always a manganese brown, yellow or orange, but sometimes green. Only rarely were they blue: this was because cobalt, used to make the blue colour and mostly obtained from the continent, was much more difficult to acquire during the latter part of the eighteenth century and the early years of the nineteenth and was therefore more expensive.

There were also larger and more sophisticated figures, some bearing characteristics of figures attributed to the Woods of Staffordshire. Some of these are classical and others are of rustic subjects.

THE MAKERS OF PRATT WARE

William Pratt and his sons Felix and John, who had potteries at Lane Delph and later at Fenton in Staffordshire, certainly made this underglaze-coloured relief-decorated ware, but there were others in the county who made similar wares. These included R. M. Astbury at Lane Delph, Richard Barker and Thomas Harley at Lane End, John and Robert Beckett at Longton, Edward Bourne, Walter Daniel and Jacob Marsh at Burslem, Jacob Tittensor at Stoke, Charles Tittensor at Shelton, Peter and Francis Warburton at Cobridge, Ralph Wedgwood and one of the Wood factories at Burslem or Brownhills.

A jug lettered Ll. VOL^NTEERS on both sides, with scenes of three soldiers presenting arms on one side and with their muskets in the firing position on the other. Made at the Leeds Pottery; c.1800. Height 155 mm.

A jug with scenes of smokers and drinkers. Another jug of identical design, but with an upswept double-scroll handle impressed WEDG-WOOD, is in the Victoria and Albert Museum; c.1795. Height 157 mm.

A full-bodied squat-shaped jug with a pronounced spout, decorated with a seated figure of Toby Fillpot drinking on one side and a scene of huntsmen at a meet on the other. Impressed FERRYBRIDGE on the base. This shape seems to be unique to Ferrybridge; c.1805. Height 117 mm.

A jug with a portrait of the Duke of York on one side and Louis XVI, Marie Antoinette and the Dauphin on the other. Heavily painted in yellow, blue and black, with portraits enclosed in medallions edged in green and ochre. Impressed HAWLEY on the base; c.1795. Height 127 mm.

Pratt ware was also made in Shropshire, Derbyshire, Yorkshire, Liverpool, Tyneside, Wearside, Scotland and even Devon. As far as is known, it was never made in Bristol or at any of the Welsh potteries.

The Leeds Pottery in Yorkshire was founded in the parish of Hunslet in 1770 by Joshua Green in partnership with his nephew John Green and Richard Humble. They made high-quality cream-coloured earthenware, some of it coloured under the glaze. Original pattern books still exist, as do some of the original moulds. The latter can be seen at the Abbey House Museum, Kirkstall, Leeds. Among these moulds are ones with portraits of Admiral Nelson and Captain Berry and also one showing Loyal Volunteers. These were both made at the Leeds Pottery. In 1820 the firm went bankrupt but struggled on through various hands until about 1880. In the late 1880s reproductions of some of the old Leeds wares were made at another pottery in Hunslet by J. W. Senior and his sons, using old moulds from the original factory. The elder Senior had worked at the old Leeds Pottery. Their wares were marketed by an enterprising antique dealer in Leeds, W. W. Slee. These pieces can easily be distinguished from the earlier ware by the fact that the colouring is over the glaze. These reproductions include the Nelson and Berry, the Loyal Volunteers, the Peace and Plenty jugs and the Macaroni tea caddy. The Seniors were in business until the 1950s.

Many other potteries in Yorkshire made underglaze-coloured ware in the eighteenth and nineteenth centuries. There were potteries at Kilnhurst, Rawmarsh, Ferrybridge and Mexborough whose imprinted marks appear on underglaze-coloured relief-decorated subjects.

At the Knottingley Pottery near Ferrybridge, 20 miles (30 km) south-east of Leeds, Josiah Wedgwood's inventive but eccentric and unbusinesslike cousin Ralph was taken into partnership in 1798. He had previously been working at the Hill Top Pottery in Burslem. There are jugs, some of them of a commemorative

Richly coloured Toby jug with a sponged base and a caryatid handle. A large crown mark is impressed on the base; c.1800-20. Height 250 mm.

Cow and calf with a farmer's wife, mounted on a sponged base. The cow is decorated with puce patches edged in black and has the same dotted eyebrows as the Toby jug, presumably from the same unidentified pottery, though it is impressed WESLEY on the base; c.1800-20. Height 153 mm.

A jug with scenes of peasants drinking and of rural musicians, both after Turner moulds. The drinking scene is after a painting by David Teniers. Impressed on the footrim HERCULANEUM above the number 18; c.1796. Height 165 mm.

nature, marked WEDGWOOD. This impressed mark does not refer to the famous Staffordshire firm of Josiah Wedgwood, for there is no evidence that they ever made this kind of ware. It is therefore likely that they were made by Ralph Wedgwood, either at Burslem or later at the Knottingley Pottery, where he worked only until 1800, when the partnership was dissolved.

The Ferrybridge firm had been entitled to use the mark WEDGWOOD & CO, but after Ralph's departure Josiah Wedgwood II objected to this. In 1805 the Knottingley Pottery changed its name to the Ferrybridge Pottery and took to using the impressed mark FERRYBRIDGE. There are many jugs of a characteristic squat shape with a deckled top that bear this mark. These are all of a good-quality cream-coloured earthenware and decorated in relief with various rustic subjects.

The Kilnhurst Old Pottery and the Top Pottery at Rawmarsh were run by Thomas and William Hawley. Both used the impressed mark HAWLEY. Some commemorative jugs, teapots and candlesticks bear this mark, as do figures of 'The Lost Sheep', the original of which has been attributed to the Woods of Staffordshire.

There is a wide range of underglaze-coloured Toby jugs and animal and figure groups of a very distinctive kind that may have come from Yorkshire. They are all of a good-quality white body and the bases are always sponged or spotted with colours, usually blue, black and ochre. Most of the subjects are unmarked, but there are some Toby jugs impressed on the base with a large crown. So far it has not been possible to identify the factory. The colours used, in addition to the usual green, brown, blue, yellow, orange and black, sometimes include a puce or raspberry colour. The same figures occur in clock groups and in cow and sheep groups.

There is one very puzzling figure of a cow with a farmer's wife in attendance that comes from this factory. It is impressed WESLEY on the base. No potter of this name is yet known, but there is a small bust of John Wesley (at the Royal Pavilion Art Gallery and Museum, Brighton) mounted on a similar sponged

White earthenware cow creamer, sponged in ochre and manganese with a milkmaid dressed in a brown blouse and yellow skirt. Mounted on a flat, shaped green-washed base. Impressed SEWELL beneath the number 7 under the base; c. 1810. Height 130 mm.

A watch stand in the form of a long-case clock, flanked by two children, coloured in orange, yellow, green and blue. Impressed on the top of the base plate DIXON, AUSTIN & CO. Made at the Garrison Pottery, Sunderland; 1820-6. Height 285 mm.

base. Did the potter, tired of making busts of the famous preacher, add the stamp to one of the cows instead? We shall probably never know.

The Herculaneum Pottery in Liverpool (1796-1804) manufactured good-quality cream-coloured earthenware. Two relief-decorated jugs, a sugar box and one teapot with the Herculaneum Pottery mark are known, though there may well be others.

In Newcastle upon Tyne there were several potteries making underglaze-coloured figures and animals. St Anthony's Pottery, run by Joseph Sewell from 1804 to 1819, made many cow creamers. Some are impressed SEWELL, some marked ST

ANTHONY; most of them are unmarked. St Peter's Pottery (Thomas Fell & Company) used the impressed mark FELL. This mark was used from 1817 to 1830. The Tyne Pottery also made cow creamers and marked its wares TAYLOR & CO. There is a wonderful display of several hundred cow creamers at the Stoke-on-Trent City Museum and Art Gallery.

The Garrison Pottery in Sunderland made underglaze-coloured figures. By 1820 the pottery was run by Robert Dixon and Thomas Austin. The mark DIXON, AUSTIN & CO was used from 1820 to 1826. It can be seen on sets of the Seasons and on some clock-group watch stands. These

9

A jug with scenes of an elopement and a Gretna Green marriage ceremony, made by Bradley & Company at Coalport and identified by sherds dug up on the site of the pottery; c.1796-1800. Height 159 mm.

figures are rather crude, but lively and brightly coloured. (See also the chapter on figures and animals.)

There are various Pratt jugs in the Royal Museum of Scotland in Edinburgh, attributed to potteries at Prestonpans, including Gordon's Bankfoot Pottery and Watson's Pottery. One particularly interesting jug is decorated in relief with a thistle in front under the spout and a pattern of ears of barley round the neck. The barley pattern occurs on many of the Scottish jugs. The quality of these east-coast wares is not quite as refined as the jugs produced in Staffordshire or Yorkshire.

The Greenock Pottery at Crawfurd's Dyke on the Clyde made classical plaques. One is marked with the incised inscription 'Greenock Pottery 1818'. Sherds from diggings near the Delftfield Pottery at Broomilaw on the north bank of the Clyde seem to indicate that the 'Parson, Clerk and Sexton' jugs were made there.

From the further evidence of pottery sherds, it is also possible to prove that a version of the 'Gretna Green Elopement and Marriage' jug was made in Shropshire by Bradley & Company of Coalport in about 1796-1800. This pottery was in business only for a very short time. It was founded by Walter Bradley with the help of William Reynolds, on whose land it was built. This was on the opposite bank of the river at Coalport from John Rose's porcelain factory.

By the 1830s the decoration of relief-moulded pottery by underglaze colouring was almost finished. However, some small potteries continued to use this process and the latest dated piece found by the authors was made by J. Emery at Mexborough in 1838. This was an extremely crude model of a long-case clock with the date and name incised on the back. After about 1820 it had become fashionable to use the brighter enamel colours, which had indeed been in use for some years. This unrestricted colour range put an end to the use of the more sober underglaze colouring.

A jug with a standing figure of Admiral Nelson set between two ships of the line and sparely painted in cobalt, brown, green, ochre and black. The same figure appears on both sides of the jug; c.1800. Height 130 mm.

COMMEMORATIVE JUGS, MUGS, FLASKS AND PLAQUES

The portraits on underglaze-coloured relief-decorated jugs, mugs, flasks and plaques often bore little resemblance to the likeness of the celebrity. The same portrait was sometimes used to portray different people. This habit continued into the 1840s, when a Staffordshire figure of Benjamin Franklin was also used for a model of George Washington.

Royalty, naval, military and political figures provide the subjects for these commemorative pieces. The Napoleonic Wars, naturally enough, produced heroes among the naval and military commanders. One of the earliest underglaze-coloured naval portraits is a mug in the form of Admiral Rodney's head, in the Victoria and Albert Museum. This is a transitional piece, part coloured glaze, part underglaze-coloured. Admiral Rodney with Admiral Hood defeated the French

off Dominica in 1782.

The naval hero most often commemorated was Admiral Lord Nelson, who appears on jugs as a full-length standing figure, as a head and shoulders portrait, as a seated figure being crowned by Neptune, and also three-dimensionally as a mug. The standing figure is taken from Lemuel Abbott's three-quarter length portrait. An engraving by William Barnard of this painting was published in 1799 and almost certainly provided the inspiration for the potters. Nelson's head and shoulders portrait had a profile of Captain Berry on the other side of the jug. Berry was Nelson's flag captain at the battle of the Nile in 1798 and served with Nelson until the admiral's death at Trafalgar in 1805.

A fine Nelson Celebration jug, versions of which can be seen at the National

11

Left: *A jug with uncoloured reliefs showing the apotheosis of Admiral Nelson, who is being drawn over the seas in a chariot by two seahorses, with Neptune crowning him. Additional relief figures of Hope, Plenty, Clio and Britannia; c.1805. Height 145 mm.*

Right: *Mug in the form of a head with 'Admiral Nelson' lettered below the rim. The initials A.G. are pencilled on the base; c.1799. Height 109 mm.*

Maritime Museum, Greenwich, has the familiar standing figure of the admiral below the spout; on one side of the jug is Britannia flanked by two soldiers and on the other side is the stern view of a man-of-war. Another rare commemorative Nelson jug has an uncoloured relief of the admiral seated in a carriage drawn by seahorses and being crowned by Neptune, and also reliefs of other classical figures. The same design of the admiral and seahorses appears on a stoneware mug marked T & J HOLLINS, who were working in Shelton from 1795 to 1820, and also appears on an unmarked smear-glazed stoneware jug banded in blue.

Among other naval commanders whose images appeared on this Pratt ware were Admiral Lord Howe, who won a great victory on the Glorious First of June in 1794, and Admiral Keppel, whose popularity with the British public owed much to his acquittal from a most unjust court-martial. His portrait, like Earl Howe's, appeared in relief on underglaze-coloured

A small, fully modelled pearlware plaque with a portrait of Admiral Jervis, Earl St Vincent. After a jasper-ware portrait medallion modelled by John de Vaere; c.1798. Height 89 mm.

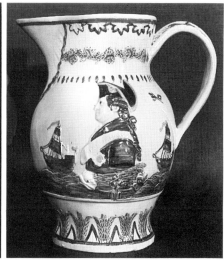

Left: *A jug with portraits of Admiral Jervis on both sides. On one side of the jug LORD JARVIS (sic) appears on scrolls on either side of his head. The admiral is set between two naval vessels. Probably made in Staffordshire, this jug is rather clumsily painted; c.1798. Height 153 mm.*

Right: *A jug with portraits of Admiral Duncan on one side and 'Captain Trolop' (sic) on the other, their names in relief on sashes across their breasts. Impressed W. DANIEL on the base. Made in Staffordshire c.1797. Height 195 mm. No blue has been used in this decoration.*

plaques. These can be seen in the Stoke-on-Trent City Museum and Art Gallery and in the National Maritime Museum at Greenwich.

Admiral Jervis was the victor of the battle of St Vincent in 1797. He is shown on a plaque, in this case copied from a jasper-ware portrait modelled by John de Vaere. His three-quarter length figure, flanked by two naval vessels, appears on jugs of various sizes and can also be found on one cast in porcelain.

Admiral Duncan won the battle of Camperdown in 1797. His profile is shown on a jug set between two naval vessels. On the reverse side of the jug is a portrait of Captain Henry Trollope, with a figure of Clio, the muse of history. Captain Trollope served under Admiral Duncan with some distinction at the battle of Camperdown, for which he was knighted. There is a handsome version of this jug impressed W. DANIEL on the base. Coarser versions of similar design are supposed to have been made at one of the

A crisply moulded octagonal jug with scenes of 'The Sailor's Return' and 'The Sailor's Farewell' on either side; c.1790. Height 180 mm.

potteries on the Scottish east coast. This is quite possible, for Duncan was a Scottish hero and had been born in Dundee. There are also some striking busts

A very fully modelled jug with relief portraits of Lord Wellington and General Hill, their names impressed below their portraits; c.1810. Height 120 mm.

A flask with portraits on one side of the ill-fated French royal family, Louis XVI, Marie Antoinette and the Dauphin, and on the other side the Duke of York; c.1794. Diameter 120 mm.

of Admiral Duncan decorated with underglaze colours.

A popular jug with naval connections was one with designs made to illustrate a set of verses called 'Jemmy's Return'. Various versions of this subject with scenes of 'The Sailor's Return' and 'The Sailor's Farewell' appear on many plaques

and jugs; some of the latter are of an attractive octagonal shape.

One of the earliest of the relief-decorated underglaze-coloured naval portraits was an oval plaque with a bust of Captain James Cook, coloured in ochre, manganese brown and blue, with the word 'Cook' incised beneath the portrait. This

A jug with a splayed foot and scalloped rim and with portraits of Queen Caroline on both sides and her name in raised letters under the rim. 'Warranted Winchester Measure' is impressed under the base; c.1820. Height 151 mm.

A jug with portraits of Thomas Denman and Henry Brougham with their names lettered in relief under the rim. The spout has the same horned satyr's head under it as does the Queen Caroline jug; c.1820. Height 105 mm.

was after a painting by William Hodges, engraved by James Basire in 1777. The design is attributed to John Flaxman. It is on view at the Wedgwood Museum, Barlaston, Staffordshire.

Military jugs and plaques include not only portraits of army commanders but scenes of military reviews and equestrian sword exercises based on engravings after paintings by Samuel Howitt, printed in 1799 in *The Sporting Magazine*. The Duke of York, the Duke of Cumberland, Lord Wellington (before he was made a duke in 1814) and Napoleon backed by a portrait of George III are all portrayed on jugs, and some on mugs as well. A jug rather crudely lettered SUCCESS TO GENERAL HARRIS was made to commemorate General Harris's victory over Tippoo Sahib at the battle of Seringapatam in 1797. The jug is impressed WEDGWOOD on the base. An attractive jug lettered LI VOLⁿTEERS shows three soldiers on one side presenting arms and on the other with their muskets in the firing position (see Introduction). This jug was made to reflect the enthusiasm for the Volunteer Forces which had been raised in 1794 to counter threats of invasion. It was probably made by the Leeds Pottery, for the same jug was reissued by the Seniors in Leeds, using old moulds, at the end of the nineteenth century.

Portraits of royalty appear on plaques, mugs, jugs and flasks. There is an oval plaque of Charles I in the Warrington Museum and Art Gallery and a companion one of Oliver Cromwell in the Wolverhampton Museum. Both these portraits are based on engravings by Charles Grignion made to illustrate *A New and Universal History of England*, published in 1787. Catherine the Great and Peter III are portrayed on a pair of plaques and they are also to be seen on a tea caddy in the Stoke-on-Trent City Museum and Art Gallery. George III is also shown on a tea caddy as well as on the verso of a jug with Napoleon on the other side. He also appears with his wife, Queen Charlotte, on a tankard.

The commonest of the royalty pieces are a series of jugs, flasks, tankards and plaques, sometimes titled 'The Royal Sufferers'. These have profile portraits of Louis XVI and Queen Marie Antoinette with the Dauphin tucked in between them. The verso of these pieces has a portrait of Frederick Augustus, Duke of York, a soldier much loved by his troops for his humanity and bravery. He was the commander of the British forces in Flanders in the victorious campaigns of 1793. A strongly coloured jug decorated with these subjects is marked HAWLEY and was made at the Kilnhurst or Rawmarsh potteries in South Yorkshire (see Introduction).

Queen Caroline, wife of George IV, wearing a feathered hat (she had a fondness for extravagant headgear), appears on plates and on a jug which has a spout decorated with a horned satyr's head. Jugs with similar spouts are lettered below the rims H. BROUGHAM ESQ M.P. and T. DENMAN ESQ M.P., with portraits in oval frames of the two lawyers who defended Queen Caroline at her trial in 1820. Portraits of Brougham and Denman also appear on plates.

Another politician who is modelled both as an underglaze-coloured equestrian figure and as a relief portrait on a jug is Sir Francis Burdett MP, who was imprisoned in the Tower of London for sedition in 1810.

A sparely coloured ovoid-shaped jug with a moulded portrait of Sir Francis Burdett MP on one side and a figure of Liberty on the other, their names impressed below; c.1810. Height 145 mm.

15

An ovoid-shaped jug with scenes of children playing on each side. MISCHIEVOUS SPORT and SPORTIVE INNOCENCE are impressed on the heart-shaped medallions; c.1795. Height 150 mm. There are white smear-glazed stoneware jugs with the same relief decoration.

SPORTING, RUSTIC AND CLASSICAL PIECES

As a change from the naval and military subjects, country sports appear widely on underglaze-coloured relief-decorated jugs and other wares. The potters must have gleaned some of their references from the sporting magazines of the day, as these were often illustrated with engravings and woodcuts.

Many sports and pastimes are illustrated, including groups of huntsmen gathering for a meet outside the local inn. Fox-hunting, deer-hunting and hare-coursing scenes are all vividly portrayed, often with the death of the unfortunate animal on one side of the piece. It did not occur to country people in those days that such pursuits might be considered cruel, although some of the more brutal activities, such as bull baiting, were made illegal in 1835. Horse racing and archery are two other country pursuits that are illustrated on underglaze-coloured jugs.

Drinking was obviously a popular subject. The three figures of the Parson, Clerk and Sexton stumbling home from a party are on a fairly common jug. There are many scenes showing topers, some resting by their horses, some at tables and some carousing in groups. Probably the most popular figure was of 'Toby Fillpot', a very fat Yorkshireman, who was reputed to have drunk more than two thousand gallons of ale in his lifetime. His likeness was copied from an engraving by Robert Dighton published in 1761. He appears on jugs as well as on many wall plaques. The latter might well have been used to decorate the parlours of inns.

Many plaques, some of considerable size, including farmyard scenes of cows, were made for the decoration of the walls of dairies and no doubt also of farmhouse kitchens. In addition there are many purely country subjects such as strutting peacocks in a landscape, birds with their nestlings or children at play.

Naive nursery rhymes were comically illustrated, such as 'Old Mother Slipper-

16

Left: A large jug decorated with hunting scenes, richly coloured in blue, green, orange, manganese brown and yellow; c.1795. Height 205 mm.
Right: A creamware jug with scenes of a smoker resting beside his horse and a befuddled toper pouring out a glass of ale. The colouring is limited to yellow, orange, green and brown; c.1795. Height 190 mm. There is a brown stoneware jug with identical scenes.

Slopper' with the old woman jumping out of bed while the fox carries off the grey goose and John, the idiotic farmhand, stands by gaping vacantly.

Classical themes were also used: Venus with her dolphin, sometimes also accompanied by Cupid; the Judgement of Paris; Diomedes and the Palladium; and a group of classically draped ladies, known as 'An Offering to Peace', from a design by Lady Templetown modelled by William Hackwood. There is another group called 'An Offering to Ceres', showing classical ladies carrying baskets of fruit and flowers. Well-modelled classically draped figures of Peace and Plenty were also popular subjects.

A small jug, made in a drab body, showing 'The Archery Lesson' on one side and two lovers on the other. The archery scene is after a Turner mould. There is a vine and ribbon border round the neck; c.1795. Height 136 mm.

17

A richly coloured jug decorated on one side with 'An Offering to Peace', after a design by Lady Templetown. The other side shows a scene of a group of three grooms drinking and smoking; c.1790. Height 180 mm.

A creamware jug, richly decorated with birds and their nestlings on one side and a landscape with a cottage and a windmill on the other. The colouring is mainly green, brown and yellow; c.1820. Height 150 mm.

18

Left: *This series of jugs is known as 'Peace and Plenty'. Peace is illustrated here. Possibly made at the Leeds Pottery to celebrate the Peace of Amiens; c.1802. Height 185 mm.*
Right: *An ovoid-shaped pearlware jug with groups of peacocks on each side, set in sunburst medallions. This is the largest of a set of five peacock-decorated jugs; c.1800. Height 230 mm. There are white smear-glazed stoneware jugs with the same relief decoration.*

An oval plaque with a deeply moulded relief figure of a boy astride a dolphin, coloured in ochre and green and framed with blue lines; c.1800. Diameter 127 mm.

19

A full-bodied jug decorated with coursing scenes. Round the neck is a vine border coloured in blue, black and green. There are traces of gilding on this example; c.1795. Height 153 mm.

A pearlware teapot, decorated with a swagged blue curtain edged with yellow. Round the base is a deep border of stiff green leaves. The top has a ring of finely moulded acanthus leaves round the lid. Impressed ASTBURY on the base; c.1790. Height 105 mm.

MISCELLANEOUS WARES

Many different objects were made with relief decoration and underglaze colouring. Among them were cups with masked faces, stirrup cups in the form of dogs' and foxes' heads, sauceboats in the most fanciful shapes including ducks, swans and mythical animals, vases, flasks, snuff bottles, cornucopias, pepperpots, tobacco jars, cradles, cruets, moneyboxes in the form of cottages and long-case clocks, pastille burners, bird feeders, pipes like men, dogs and snakes, candlesticks, love tokens, tea caddies, tea and coffee pots and Toby jugs.

Of the four teapots illustrated here, three have the maker's name impressed upon the base. The first, the one without a lid, is impressed ASTBURY. This was the mark used by Richard Meir Astbury (1765-1834), who succeeded his father, Joshua Astbury, at the Foley Works, Lane Delph. The second, which has a painted land-scape on it in the manner of the painting on Dutch tiles, is marked BARKER. There were Barkers potting at the end of the eighteenth century in both Staffordshire and Yorkshire. The Staffordshire Barkers had a pottery in Lane End; the Yorkshire Barkers had potteries in Mexborough and Rawmarsh. This teapot might have come from any of these potteries. The third marked teapot is decorated with unusual relief figures of women churning butter, pouring out tea and carrying a basket. It is impressed both under the lid and on the base with C. GRESLEY. This stands for Church Gresley in Derbyshire. There were a number of potteries there and it is not certain which one used this mark.

In the Bulwer Collection of teapots in the Castle Museum at Norwich there is a splendid array of teapots, many of them decorated with underglaze colouring.

A small pepperpot in the form of a bust

21

A six-sided pearlware teapot decorated on one side with a small figure of Mercury within an oval frame and on the other with a seated classical figure. The designs are flanked by yellow vertical panels. The lid has a swan finial; c.1800. Height 170 mm.

A teapot decorated on both sides with the same relief designs. There is stiff yellow and green leaf decoration round the top and the lid has an orange-coloured lion finial. Impressed C. GRESLEY; c.1800. Height 170 mm.

A teapot with a small landscape painted in blue, green, brown, yellow and ochre in central panels on each side. The lid is surmounted with a dolphin knob and set within a crenellated gallery. Impressed BARKER on the base. Made in Staffordshire or Yorkshire; c.1790. Height 165 mm.

of a woman is an unusual piece. Her broad-brimmed black hat has perforations in the crown to allow the pepper to fall through. Her colouring and the sponged waisted socle suggest that she comes from the pottery that used the impressed crown mark.

The tea caddy with Macaroni figures is one of the commoner pieces of Pratt ware. The one shown here is coloured only in blue but most examples are fully coloured in blue, orange, yellow, green, brown and black. The tollhouse moneybox, because of its sponged base and strong colouring, may also have come from the pottery that used the impressed crown mark, as does the long-case clock moneybox.

Of the other pieces illustrated in this chapter, the most interesting are the Toby jugs and the Bacchus and Pan jug. The Toby jug with the impressed crown on its base has already been discussed in the Introduction. Of the other three Toby jugs illustrated here, the one in the middle of the group is a coloured-glaze model, probably from one of the Wood factories. The other two are underglaze-coloured and both of them hold brown tankards. The Bacchus and Pan jug is vividly decorated in strong underglaze colours. The seated figure of Bacchus is back to back with the standing god Pan. The original

of this jug is said to come from one of the Wood factories and was decorated with coloured glazes. The underglaze-coloured version is much more striking. There is a similar one in the Yorkshire Museum at York impressed HAWLEY.

A tea caddy with Macaroni figures in relief of a bewigged gentleman and his servant on one side and a lady with an elaborate headdress and her maid on the other; coloured only in blue; c.1780. Height 112 mm.

Left: *A pepperpot in the form of the bust of a woman, draped in yellow, orange and blue and wearing a black hat with a perforated crown. Mounted on a waisted socle sponged in orange and blue; c.1800-20. Height 105 mm.*

Right: *A circular moneybox with a slit in the roof, in the form of a tollhouse. Coloured in blue, orange and green with a sponged base; c.1810. Height 120 mm.*

A group of Toby jugs. The Toby in the centre is a coloured-glaze Ralph Wood model. The ones on either side are underglaze-coloured in brown, ochre, blue, black and yellow; c.1780-1810. Height 242 mm.

24

A moneybox in the form of a long-case clock flanked by male and female figures and with a spaniel at the foot of the clock. This spaniel often appears between the feet of those Toby jugs that are marked with an impressed crown. The base is sponged in black, blue and orange; c.1800-20. Height 220 mm.

Bacchus jug, based on a Ralph Wood model and vividly coloured in green, ochre, yellow, brown and blue. Bacchus is sitting on a wine barrel. On the verso is the god Pan. The spout should be in the form of a dolphin but has been damaged and clumsily repaired; c.1800-20. Height 290 mm.

25

A group of underglaze-coloured 'toy' figures, some showing arbitrary painting with blobs of ochre, manganese and blue; c.1785-1800. Heights 95-130 mm.

FIGURES AND ANIMALS

The most primitive of the underglaze-coloured figures are the small 'toys' made from simple two-piece moulds. These mostly come from Staffordshire. A pair depicting a farmer and his wife shows two little figures seated on tree trunks and nursing a cockerel and a dog. The man has an ochre-coloured coat; the woman's dress is decorated with manganese brown blobs. This style of spotted decoration was used on many of these small figures. It is impossible to say who made them, but various potters were listed in contemporary directories as 'toy makers'. An invoice from Ralph Wood dated 16th November 1783 (after an order from Josiah and Thomas Wedgwood) was for 'Six doz small coloured figures 18d a doz = 9s'. A penny halfpenny does not seem an exorbitant amount for one of these attractive little figures.

Very few of the larger and more sophisticated underglaze-coloured figures are marked. Some rather clumsy figures are marked TITTENSOR. This mark probably refers to Charles Tittensor, who was working in Hanley in the early years of the nineteenth century. A handsome set of the four Seasons comes from the Garrison Pottery in Sunderland. These figures are impressed DIXON, AUSTIN & CO. This partnership was in existence from 1820 to 1826. A figure of a fisher girl is marked with a pencilled cursive 'Jacob Marsh' under the base. This refers to a potter who was working in the early nineteenth century at Burslem and later at Lane Delph.

There are many unmarked underglaze-coloured figures, often of classical origin, such as Faith, Hope and Charity, Venus, Mercury, Flora and Apollo, and so on.

The figure of Mercury illustrated here was inspired by an early sixteenth-century terracotta figure by Giovanna di Bologna. The two figures of Amphitrite are also probably after terracottas by the same sculptress. Some of the classical figures are after models attributed to the Woods.

The girl holding an apron full of fruit is referred to as Iphigenia; she is thought to be a Ralph Wood model. She is usually partnered by the figure of an uncouth young man known as Simon. These characters are taken from Boccaccio's *Decameron*.

The two figures kissing each other under the shade of an umbrella are perhaps from the same pottery that made the cow group impressed WESLEY. The blue spots surrounded by puce circles on the girl's dress are exactly the same as those on the dress worn by the farmer's wife in the Wesley group.

Some lively and strongly coloured figures were produced in Yorkshire. Rather primitive figures with this kind of colouring were made by the Leeds Pottery. The same pottery produced very large horses, specially made for saddlers and druggists to display in their windows.

Many animals in the form of simple 'toys' were made and these include squirrels, bears, foxes and dogs. Among larger pieces were deer, sheep, horses and goats and large cockerels with detachable heads. Many naive cow creamers were produced, particularly by the Tyneside potteries (see Introduction). In the Stoke-on-Trent City Museum and Art Gallery, in addition to a wonderful great herd of cow creamers, there are two amusing and brightly coloured lions, standing on elaborate bases and wearing mournful expressions. In the same museum there is also a strange creature with a sheep's head, a fish's body and a cockerel's tail. It is in the form of a container and the dorsal fin serves as a handle to the lid. It is known as 'Neither fish, flesh, fowl or good red herring'.

A powerful bull-baiting group can be found decorated with underglaze colours, sponged on both the animal and its green base. The flanks of the creature are also

A set of the Seasons, possibly after Wood models, decorated in particularly strong deep cobalt, yellow, burnt orange, mossy green and black. Impressed DIXON, AUSTIN & CO. Made at the Garrison Pottery, Sunderland; c.1820-6. Height 217 mm.

27

Figure of a fisher girl, holding a basket of blue fish. Her dress is spotted with brown and edged with ochre. The square base is marbled with blue lines and pencilled beneath is 'Jacob Marsh', whose pottery was in Burslem; c.1790-1800. Height 127 mm.

Left: Hermes or Mercury, the winged messenger. His tunic is spotted in ochre and brown. His helmet is of the same colours and he stands against a green-washed support; c.1800. Height 190 mm.

Two figures of Venus, each with a green-washed dolphin at her side. One figure is spotted in brown and ochre and the other is coloured in yellow, burnt orange, blue and manganese; c.1800. Heights 145 and 149 mm.

decorated with orange and manganese circles. A version of this bull-baiting group was listed in one of John Wood's account books: 'Two coloured bulls with dogs 1.8d'. There is a good example of this group in the Stoke-on-Trent City Museum. Animals such as these were made to sell at 10d each. Little did the potters who made them realise that within two centuries they would be sold for hundreds of pounds.

'The Umbrella Courtship': two figures kissing under a brown umbrella. The man has a black hat and a blue frock-coat edged with ochre. The girl has a bonnet trimmed with puce. They stand on a green base; c.1810. Height 140 mm.

Figure of Iphigenia wearing a yellow dress with a flower-patterned underskirt in blue and ochre. She is mounted on a tapered square base with a border of ochre and yellow stiff leaves; c.1790. Height 241 mm.

Bull-baiting group after one of the Wood designs. The bull is sponged in manganese, with brown and orange circles on his sides and back. The dog is spotted in brown and orange. Mounted on a green sponged rocky base; c.1790. Height 203 mm.

A sheep, blotched in burnt orange, standing on a green mound in front of a tree trunk in the form of a spill vase. A lamb rests at her feet. Her fleece is impressed with small circles with a dot in the centre; c.1785. Height 135 mm.

31

FURTHER READING

Lawrence, Heather. *Yorkshire Pots and Potteries*. David & Charles, Newton Abbot, 1974.

Lewis, Griselda. *A Collector's History of English Pottery*. Antique Collectors' Club, Woodbridge, fourth edition 1987.

Lewis, John and Griselda. *Pratt Ware. English and Scottish Relief Decorated and Underglaze Coloured Earthenware, 1780-1840*. Antique Collectors' Club, Woodbridge, 1984.

McVeigh, Patrick. *Scottish East Coast Potteries 1750-1840*. John Donald, Edinburgh, 1979.

Rhead, G. W. *The Earthenware Collector*. Herbert Jenkins, London, 1920.

PLACES TO VISIT

The following museums have collections of Pratt ware. Museum displays may be altered and readers are advised to telephone before making a special journey, to check that the Pratt ware is on display, and to find out the opening times.

GREAT BRITAIN

Abbey House Museum, Kirkstall, Leeds, West Yorkshire LS5 3GH. Telephone: 0532 755821.

British Museum, Great Russell Street, London WC1B 3DG. Telephone: 071-636 1555.

Castle Museum, Norwich, Norfolk NR1 3JU. Telephone: 0603 223624.

Doncaster Museum and Art Gallery, Chequer Road, Doncaster, South Yorkshire DN1 2AE. Telephone: 0302 734293.

Fitzwilliam Museum, Trumpington Street, Cambridge CB2 1RB. Telephone: 0223 332900. The Glaisher Collection.

National Maritime Museum, Romney Road, Greenwich, London SE10 9NF. Telephone: 081-858 4422.

Royal Museum of Scotland, Chambers Street, Edinburgh EH1 1JF. Telephone: 031-225 7534.

Royal Pavilion Art Gallery and Museum, 4/5 Pavilion Buildings, Brighton, East Sussex BN1 1UE. Telephone: 0273 603005.

Stoke-on-Trent City Museum and Art Gallery, Bethesda Street, Hanley, Stoke-on-Trent, Staffordshire ST1 3DE. Telephone: 0782 202173.

Temple Newsam House, Leeds, West Yorkshire LS15 0AE. Telephone: 0532 647321 or 641358.

Victoria and Albert Museum, Cromwell Road, South Kensington, London SW7 2RL. Telephone: 071-938 8500.

Walker Art Gallery, William Brown Street, Liverpool, Merseyside L3 8EL. Telephone: 051-207 0001.

UNITED STATES OF AMERICA

Colonial Williamsburg, Goodwin Building, Williamsburg, Virginia 23185.

Mint Museum of Art, 2730 Randolph Road, Charlotte, North Carolina 28207. The Delhom Gallery.

Nelson-Atkins Museum of Art, 4525 Oak Street, Kansas City, Missouri 64111. The Burnap Collection.